The Sioux Indians

by Bill Lund

Content Consultant:
Dave Meyer
Creative Technician, Development Office
St. Joseph's Indian School

Bridgestone Books

an imprint of Capstone Press

Bridgestone Books are published by Capstone Press
818 North Willow Street, Mankato, Minnesota 56001
http://www.capstone-press.com

Library of Congress Cataloging-in-Publication Data
Lund, Bill, 1954-
    The Sioux Indians/by Bill Lund.
    p. cm.--(Native peoples)
    Includes bibliographical references and index.
    Summary: Provides an overview of the past and present lives of the Sioux, or Dakota,
Indians, covering their daily life, customs, relations with the government and others, and more.
    ISBN 1-56065-563-1
    1. Dakota Indians--History--Juvenile literature. 2. Dakota Indians--Social life and
customs--Juvenile literature.
    [1. Dakota Indians. 2. Indians of North America--Great Plains.] I. Title.
    II. Series: Lund, Bill, 1954-   Native peoples.

E99.D1L86 1998
978'.0049752--dc21

                                        97-6394
                                         CIP
                                          AC

Photo credits
Lakota Cultural Center, 8, 20
Oglala Lakota College, 16
Cheyenne Rouse, cover
St. Joseph Indian School, 6, 14
Faith A. Uridel, 10, 12
Brian A. Vikander, 18

Table of Contents

Map

Canada

U.S.A.

Mexico

Where the Sioux used to live

Fast Facts

Today, many Sioux Indians live like most other North Americans. In the past, they practiced a different way of life. Their food, homes, and clothing helped make them special. These facts tell how the Sioux once lived.

Food: The Sioux ate buffalo meat. They also ate meat from other animals they hunted. They gathered fruits and vegetables, too.

Home: The Sioux lived in tepees. Tepees were made of poles. The poles were covered with animal skins.

Clothing: Most Sioux clothing was made from buffalo skins. They wore leggings, shirts, dresses, and vests. They also wore moccasins and gloves.

Language: The Sioux language is part of the Siouian language family.

Past Location: The Sioux once lived in the area of Minnesota, North Dakota, South Dakota, and Wisconsin. Some also lived along the Mississippi river and in Manitoba, Canada.

Current Location: Today, the Sioux live on reservations in Minnesota, Nebraska, North Dakota, and South Dakota.

Special Events: Sacred Pipe ceremonies are important to the Sioux. A ceremony is an official practice. The Sioux also hold powwows. A powwow is a gathering for Native Americans.

5

The Sioux People

The Sioux have lived on the Great Plains for hundreds of years. They lived in the area of Minnesota, North Dakota, South Dakota, and Wisconsin. Some lived along the Mississippi river. Others lived in southern Manitoba, Canada.

The Sioux Nation is very large. A nation is a group of people. These people have similar language, customs, and government. Seven tribes make up the Sioux Nation. A tribe is similar to a nation but smaller. Sioux tribes are the Mdewakanton, Sisseton, Teton, Wahpekute, Wahpeton, Yankton, and Yanktonai. The Teton tribe is made up of seven smaller groups.

Sometimes the Sioux fought with other nations. One nation gave them the name Sioux. It means snake or enemy. The U.S. government learned this name. It still calls them Sioux today.

Today, some Sioux live on reservations. A reservation is land set aside for Native Americans.

The Sioux still remember their traditions.

7

Homes, Food, and Clothing

Until the early 1800s, many buffalo lived on the Great Plains. The Great Plains are in the Midwest. The Sioux were skilled at hunting buffalo. They used every part of the buffalo.

The Sioux lived in tepees made from buffalo skins. A tepee was made of poles. The poles formed a cone-shaped triangle. Buffalo skins were stretched over the poles. A tepee could be taken down and moved easily.

Sioux women made jerky by drying buffalo meat. They pounded the dried meat into a powder. Then they added berries and melted fat to the powder. They called jerky pemmican. It could be stored for many years.

The Sioux made clothes and blankets from buffalo skins. The men wore leggings and shirts. The women wore dresses. Both men and women wore moccasins. Winters were cold. The Sioux wore gloves and heavy robes to stay warm.

The Sioux lived in tepees made from buffalo skins.

Star Quilts

Star quilts are important to the Sioux. A quilt is a warm blanket for a bed. Often it is thick and padded. Star quilts remind the Sioux of how a community works. Each piece of the quilt is like a person. Every piece is different. Each piece is necessary to make the quilt whole.

The Sioux use thread to hold the quilt together. Thread is like friendships. They feel it is important to keep friendships strong. Strong friendships hold a community together.

Sioux women make the quilts. They use many different colors. The pieces are also made of different patterns. The Sioux give star quilts as gifts for special occasions.

The Sioux give star quilts as gifts.

The Sioux Family

Long ago, family groups often lived together in one tepee. A family group is parents and children. It can also include grandparents, aunts, and uncles. Many family groups lived in a village.

Children are very important to the Sioux. In the past, parents held ceremonies for newborn babies. A ceremony is a special event. A respected adult breathed into a newborn baby's mouth. The Sioux believed this was good for the baby. It passed on some of the adult's goodness.

Children learned from adults. Older men taught young boys to hunt. Older women taught young girls to make clothing. The women also taught girls to prepare food.

Today, many Sioux children go to reservation schools. They learn the same subjects as other North American children. They also learn about Sioux traditions. A tradition is a practice continued over many years.

Children are very important to the Sioux.

The Sacred Pipe Religion

The Sioux have a traditional religion. A religion is a set of beliefs people follow. The Sioux religion is called the Sacred Pipe religion. The Great Spirit is the Sioux God. They also believe in a spirit called White Buffalo Calf Woman. She gave them a sacred pipe. The Sioux smoke tobacco with the pipe. Each tribe has a pipe.

Sometimes, Sioux men offered tobacco in a pipe to religious leaders. This meant that the man wanted to begin a vision ceremony. This ceremony included fasting. Fasting means to give up eating for a time. The person fasting hoped to receive a vision. A vision is a dream. The vision told the person fasting how to live.

Some Sioux still practice the Sacred Pipe religion. Others follow the Christian religion. Christianity is a religion based on the teachings of Christ. Many Sioux practice both the Sacred Pipe and Christian religions.

Each tribe has a sacred pipe.

Sioux Government

Long ago, the Sioux lived in villages. Each village had a chief. The chief was chosen because he was a strong leader. The chief helped the village make important decisions.

The adult men in each village formed a council. This council discussed problems. Then they made decisions for the village.

Each village had several groups of men. The chief chose one group each year. The chosen group made sure people obeyed the law.

Sometimes Sioux villages joined together to hunt or to fight wars. The joined villages were called a tribe. There were seven main tribes. All seven tribes together were known as the Seven Council Fires. Each tribe had a tribal chief.

Today, the Sioux have reservation governments. Each reservation has a tribal council. The council chairperson is like a chief. He or she helps make decisions for the reservation.

A chairperson helps make decisions for the tribe.

Sioux Battles

Many Sioux once lived in the Black Hills of South Dakota. The U.S. government signed treaties that promised the Black Hills to the Sioux. A treaty is an official agreement between two nations. But gold was discovered in the Black Hills. The U.S. government broke the treaty. It took the land from the Sioux.

In 1876, the Sioux fought to keep their land. They fought the Battle of the Little Bighorn. U.S. Army Colonel George Custer ordered his troops to attack. A man named Crazy Horse led the Sioux. Custer and most of his army died.

In 1890, the U.S. Army and the Sioux fought again. This is known as the Battle of Wounded Knee. It is also called the Wounded Knee Massacre. No one is sure how the battle started. One of the Sioux might have fired his gun by mistake. The army started firing at the Sioux. This time, many Sioux died.

The Sioux fought to keep their land.

How the Sioux Began

The Sioux told many stories called legends. Legends often explained things in nature. One legend tells how the Sioux people began.

Many years ago, the Great Spirit sent a huge flood. Everyone drowned except for one woman. She climbed to a high cliff. Then she called out to the Great Spirit. She asked the Great Spirit to save her. She held her hands up to the sky. The Great Spirit sent a big eagle down to her.

The woman grabbed the eagle's claws. The eagle carried her to safety in the Black Hills. When the eagle landed, he turned into a man. This man and the woman had children. Their children became the Sioux nation.

Today, storytellers still tell Sioux legends.

Hands On: Make a Calendar

The Sioux used a calendar to remember important events. Their calendars were made of pictures instead of words. The Sioux made pictures of battles and hunts. They also made pictures to remember births and deaths. You can make a calendar, too.

What You Need

markers, crayons, pens, or pencils
paper

What You Do

1. Write down important events that have happened since you were born. An important event could be the birth of a new sister or brother. Your first day of school or fun vacations are also important.
2. Draw each of these events onto your piece of paper.
3. Keep adding pictures of important events to the calendar. This calendar will help you remember these events. You can also use it to tell stories about your life.

Words to Know

fast (FAST)—to give up eating for a time
nation (NAY-shuhn)—a group of people with the same language, customs, and government
pemmican (PEM-mi-can)—dried buffalo meat that is mixed with berries and melted fat
reservation (rez-ur-VAY-shuhn)—land set aside for use by Native Americans
tepee (TEE-pee)—a house made of poles that are covered by animal skins
tradition (truh-DISH-uhn)—a practice continued over many years

Read More

Landau, Elaine. *The Sioux*. New York: Franklin Watts, 1989.
Osinski, Alice. *The Sioux*. Chicago: Children's Press, 1992.
Sneve, Virginia Driving Hawk. *The Sioux*. New York: Holiday House, 1993.

Useful Addresses

Flandreau Santee Sioux
Flandreau Field Office
Box 283
Flandreau, SD 57028

Sisseton-Wahpeton Sioux
Route 2, Agency Village
Sisseton, SD 57262

Internet Sites

Native American Cultural Resources on the Internet
http://hanksville.phast.umass.edu/misc/
NAculture.html

A Guide to the Great Sioux Nation
http://www.state.sd.us/state/executive/tourism/
sioux/sioux.htm

Index